DEDICATION

I dedicate this book to all young boys and girls around the world who struggle with stuttering or any disability. You are not your disability; it does not define who you are. You define yourself and who you want to be. If you can believe it, you can achieve it.

ACKNOWLEDGMENT PAGE

I would like to acknowledge all those who have SUPPORTED, ENCOURAGED, and PUSHED me to strive for excellence in all that I do. First, I would like to thank God for always being there to keep me focused on what's important in life. Next to my Mother, Father and Stepparents who endlessly show their love without hesitation to invest in my future by presenting me with opportunities like this. To all my brothers and sisters for their support. And to the teachers, who willingly and effortlessly convey their suggestive skills of education to see me and other kids improve. Without their continuous love, care, and prayers, my progress would not have been possible. Thanks to everyone who had a hand in my upbringing, Thank you!

Honorable Mentions:

Falon A. Timmons
Stephen R. Moss
Tavares C. Timmons
Neha H Moss
Shamonti C.Timmons
Tavares C. Timmons jr.
Editor Valerie Pugh-Love
Mrs. William Hall
Ms. Concepcion J.

"Mom, mom it's almost t-t-time to go to the caterpillar speech p-p-pathologist. I c-c-can't wait! We've been planning this for months."

"Jimmy! What time is it?" his mom asked as she glanced at the alarm clock.

"It's 5:30 a.m.," he replied.

Your appointment isn't until 12 o'clock."

Jimmy left his mom alone and drifted back to sleep.

"Jimmy, it's time to wake up. We're leaving in thirty minutes," his mom said.

After what seemed like a short nap, he noticed that it was now just an hour before his appointment.

As Jimmy scurried out of bed and started to get dressed, he heard the doorbell ring. He wondered who that could be!

"Who is it?"

"It's Mr. Scurry," an unfamiliar voice responded.

"How may I help you?" Jimmy's mom asked.

"I'm looking for Jimmy," he replied.

"I heard Jimmy's cries. He called for me, so I scurried to his rescue. I'm a speech pathologist, and I'm here to help him with his stuttering."

Jimmy crouched behind the stairs thinking, " What a strange caterpillar!"

When Mr. Scurry spotted him, he told Jimmy to come out.

"What type of caterpillar are you?" Jimmy asked as he stood on the stairs.

"I'm the speech pathologist that you have been asking for. Let's go on an adventure, and I will tell you all about my special powers. I'm taking you out to show you how some things you view as problems aren't problems at all."

"Well, my stuttering is a problem. The kids at school and Leaf Field will not pick me for any games. On top of that, they're always making fun of me!"

Mr. Scurry wrapped his wings that looked like a cape around Jimmy's shoulders. Suddenly, they both disappeared. When they reappeared at a park, Jimmy wondered how Mr. Scurry made them disappear.

"Wait, Jimmy. Look over there," Mr. Scurry said, as he pointed toward the trees. "There is so much more to this than you think. Look! A kid needs your help! How about you go help him?"

Jimmy replied, "I would love to help!"

When he looked around, Mr. Scurry was nowhere to be found. So, he walked over to the beetle that was holding a stick.

"What's your name? My name is Jimmy."

"My name is Beetle-Chase."

"W-w-what's that stick you're holding in your hand? Are you okay?" Jimmy asked.

Beetle-Chase explained, "I'm okay. I'm blind; this stick is my guide,"

"How are you okay and you're blind?" Jimmy asked.

"My life is amazing in every way! That's because I have my stick. I call him White Cane. Many people like myself who are blind or visually impaired use a white cane. White Cane allows us to scan our surroundings for obstacles or orientation marks. It is also helpful for onlookers to identify us as blind or visually impaired and take appropriate care with us. Jimmy, my blindness is not a problem at all. You see, I was born this way. My stick is to me what your eyes are to you - a guide. I love my life the way it is."

Suddenly, Beetle-Chase was long gone, and Mr. Scurry had reappeared. Jimmy wondered where Mr. Scurry had gone. Before he could ask, Mr. Scurry said, "Are you ready to continue our adventure?"

"Yes. Where are you taking me this time?" Before Jimmy could get an answer, they quickly disappeared and were off to the next adventure.

While swiftly moving through the air, Mr. Scurry asked, "What bothers you most about stuttering, Jimmy?"

"I don't like getting bullied at Leaf Field. When kids repeat me, it makes me angry, nervous, and f-f-frustrated."

"Maybe this situation can help you with your stutter."

Before Jimmy could answer, he spotted an ant alone by a pile of stone rocks.

"Hello," Jimmy said. The ant did not turn around, so Jimmy tapped him on his shoulder and greeted him again.

The ant said, "Hello," and smiled as he moved his hands and fingers. "My name is George," said the ant while still moving his hands and fingers.

"Are you okay?" Jimmy asked. "Why are you moving your hands and fingers?"

George replied. "I'm deaf. This is sign language. It helps me communicate with you."

"What do you mean you're deaf? You were just talking to me."

"I can't hear, but I can read your mouth movements."

"Wow! That is amazing! I wish I could do that."

"I have progressive hearing loss. I can hear a little with a hearing aid. My audiologist tells me that I'm not completely deaf. When I was little, I learned to read lips. I also use sign language, which is a language for the hearing impaired. I learned to sign at a very early age and most of my spoken
vocabulary comes from learning new words through reading.
English has so many words that just aren't spoken the way they are spelled, but I manage."

George then showed Jimmy some sign language, and then they played a little while.

Moments after Jimmy's conversation with George, he could feel Mr. Scurry standing right next to him. He was still puzzled about where Mr. Scurry disappeared to, but he did not ask any questions. They continued their journey despite Jimmy's wandering mind.

As they walked, Jimmy saw a leaf-cream truck and asked if he could get one.

Mr. Scurry said, "Why sure."

When Jimmy realized that he had no money, he turned around and asked Mr. Scurry for a green leaf. Once again, he was gone, but he left a green leaf floating in the air. Jimmy picked up the green leaf and bought a strawberry grape bean ice-leaf cone.

Seconds before he took the first lick of his cone, he noticed that a caterpillar had dropped her grape ice-leaf cone. So, Jimmy walked over and shared his leaf-cream with her. She thanked him for his kindness, and they started talking to each other.

"My name is Lily."

Before Jimmy could introduce himself, Lily heard Yellow Jacket bullying other kids.

Jimmy asked, "Wh-o-o is that?"

"That's Yellow Jacket!" Lily replied as she and Jimmy walked over to the playground.

"This is a p-park for everyone," Lilly stuttered.

Yellow Jacket froze and then started to laugh.

"You need to stop b-b-bullying! That's not nice!" Said Lily.

Jimmy suddenly realized that Lily had a speech impairment just like he did.

"You and I both stutter?" Jimmy asked.

"I s-s-sure do, I have been stuttering since I can remember, but I manage to get through my words ju-ust fine when I'm not so angry. I can't stand to see someone bully someone else." Said Lilly.

"I used to get bullied a lot, but I stood up for myself one day."

"How did you do that?" Asked Jimmy.

"I just explained that there is nothing wrong with me. I'm just like the rest of the kids; I just stutter."

Jimmy felt motivated by Lily and planned to stand up for himself just the same.

"Let's play soccer," Lily said.

"First, let me show you a trick."

Jimmy kicked the ball up into the air and scored a goal. Lily applauded and then they played a game of soccer. She showed her new friend a few tricks of her own before they took a break.

While taking a break, they spotted Skunky bullying Yellow Jacket.

They walked over and told Skunky to leave him alone. Yellow Jacket was surprised that they stood up for him.

They asked Yellow Jacket if he wanted to play a game of soccer with them.

He asked, "Why are you helping me after what I did to you?" Jimmy replied "no one should be bullied."

Yellow Jacket apologized for being mean, and they all enjoyed several games of soccer together.

As they played, Jimmy heard the faint sounds of his mom's voice. "Jimmy... Jimmy..."

"Jimmy, wake up... Jimmy, wake up. It's time for your appointment," his mom said while rubbing his head.

He awakened, and said, "Mom, I just had the best dream ever."

"Okay, son. Tell me all about it on the way to your appointment."

When they arrived at their appointment, Jimmy noticed that his speech pathologist resembled Mr. Scurry.

"That's Mr. Scurry!" Jimmy exclaimed.

"Who is Mr. Scurry?" His mom replied.

"The speech pathologist."

"No, Jimmy. His name is Mr. Hurry."

Just then Mr. Hurry walked in and introduced himself. "My name is Mr. Hurry. What's yours?" He asked.

"I'm Jimmy."

"Hi, Jimmy. I will be telling you what speech is. We'll mostly talk about why you are struggling in speech, and we will focus on helping you control your stutter on our appointment visits,
because I hear you are struggling in speech. To improve, you must speak slowly and clearly. Take your time and breathe. When you go home, practice conversations so you can get better."

After they talked about slowing down when speaking, Mr. Hurry gave Jimmy a sheet of paper with fluency enhancing
behaviors on it. They went over the behaviors. They discussed "light contact" which means touching the articulators in the mouth and lips together very lightly and softly when speaking. "Slow rate" means to speak very slowly and easily.

"Thank you, Jimmy, for our session today. When you go home, practice by reading a book slowly so you won't stutter."

As Jimmy and his mom got ready to leave, Mr. Hurry yelled Jimmy's name. He looked back, and Mr. Hurry winked at him. Then, he saw Mr. Scurry's cape-like wing again and smiled. Over time and with much practiced, Jimmy's speech improved thanks to his new friend.

After school one day, Jimmy's mom asked, "How was your day?"

With confidence he said, "My speech was perfect today."

She replied with a smile, "You've changed.

"Yes, Mom. I have my wings. Besides, you always said that we are fearfully and wonderfully made, and I know it now!"

LETTER FROM THE AUTHOR

Dear Readers,

Thanks to all who purchase this book. To anyone who thinks that their disability takes purpose away from their life's choices, let me tell you that it doesn't.

That is just what I thought.

You are your own person, and you decide what goes on in your life. I hope you enjoyed reading the book.

It was inspired by my life's story.

Sincerely,

Stephen R. Moss, Jr.

RESOURCES

Here is a list of Resources that will help you and your child along their journey to improve:

1. National stutter Association:
www.westutter.org

2. National Institute on deafness & other communication Disorders (NIDCD): www.nidcd.nih.gov/heath/stuttering

3. Author's website
www.stutter-fly.com

4. Your Child's School
Contact the main office to get information about Speech Therapy.

VOCABULARY TERMS

Articulator: any of the vocal organs above the larynx, including the tongue, lips, teeth, and hard palate.

Audiologist: A health care professional who is trained to evaluate hearing loss and related disorders

Auditory Perception: the ability to identify, interpret, and attach meaning to sound.

Blindness: a lack of vision; also refers to a loss of vision that cannot be corrected with glasses or contact lenses.

Fluency Enhancing Behaviors: strategies include skills such as Relaxed Breathing, Slow Stretched Speech, Smooth Movement, Easy Voice, Light Contact, and Stretched Speech.

Resembled: have qualities or features, especially those of appearance, in common with (someone or something); look or seem like.

Stutter: also known as stammering; a speech disorder in which the flow of speech is disrupted by involuntary repetitions and prolongations of sounds, syllables, words, or phrases as well as involuntary silent pauses or blocks

Speech Impairment: a condition in which the ability to produce speech sounds that are necessary to communicate with others is impaired.

Speech Pathologist: a specialist who evaluates and treats patients with speech, language, cognitive-communication, and swallowing disorders in individuals of all ages, from infants to the elderly.

Sign Language: a system of communication using visual gestures and signs, as used by deaf people.

Unfamiliar: not known or recognized

Swiftly: at high speed or quickly.

Obstacles: a thing that blocks one's way or prevents or hinders progress.

Orientation marks: knowing where you are and being able to plan how to go where you want to be. Mobility is the actual movement from place to place. Together, orientation and mobility are commonly referred to as " O&M ."

White Cane: a device used by many people who are blind or visually impaired. A white cane primarily allows its user to scan their surroundings for obstacles or orientation marks; also helpful for onlookers in identifying the user as blind or visually impaired and taking appropriate care.

Made in United States
North Haven, CT
16 July 2024

54866683R10020